T0354967

HUMBLE PAIN

PRISILLA CONCEPCION

WESTBOW
PRESS®
A DIVISION OF THOMAS NELSON
& ZONDERVAN

WestBow Press books may be ordered through booksellers or by contacting:

WestBow Press
A Division of Thomas Nelson & Zondervan
1663 Liberty Drive
Bloomington, IN 47403
www.westbowpress.com
844-714-3454

ISBN: 978-1-6642-1746-1 (sc)
ISBN: 978-1-6642-1748-5 (hc)
ISBN: 978-1-6642-1747-8 (e)

Library of Congress Control Number: 2020925385

Print information available on the last page.

WestBow Press rev. date: 12/22/2020

ENCOURAGEMENT FROM OTHERS

Angel Rivera (Florida)

In my senior year of high school, I found out that I had an injury that had been affecting my body for years. I barely was able to walk at times. Being in that hospital had me questioning so much. Why was I just now finding out about this? How different could my life have been had I figured it all out earlier? How was I going to move forward with my life after all of this? Was I going to be able to even walk across that stage to graduate?

All those questions got answered. God showed me that even through an injury that was so rare no doctor had seen it before, he pushed me with strength to walk a path that he made and cleared for me. And all those questions of "What next?" were answered as I was able to walk across the stage and grab my diploma. I now have been provided with better strength today than I've ever had. Though the walk is never easy, Christ will provide strength.

Instagram profile: @ riivvera.a

Ben Orleus (Florida)

The most painful experience I went through was my father's passing. At a young age, and this being my first experience with the death of a loved one, I was confused and became mad at God. I did not know that hope and a future come through pain. With me being the only male left in my immediate family, this experience that God took me through ended up humbling me. Throughout the years, I have learned how my father was as a man, and now I am creating a future for my mother, siblings, and future family, in honor of him.

Instagram profile: @ _rookswrld_

PREFACE

Hello, everyone! My name is Prisilla Concepcion, and most of you have found me on social media platforms such as Instagram. I'd like to give a special thanks to all of those who have shown support during this writing process.

During my whole entire life, I have struggled with depression. I have always been so hurt and upset because my father, Ricardo Concepcion, has been in prison since I was just two years old. He was misguided and followed the wrong path in life. It doesn't define who he is because although he has been distant, we have a very close relationship, unlike many people who physically *live* with their fathers! It's a blessing and a curse.

One day, God placed in my heart the idea to create something beautiful out of an ugly situation. So that's when I started creating *Humble Pain*. This book is for people who have loved ones who are incarcerated, to inspire them to create beauty out of ashes. This book is for those who struggle with depression and anxiety. I have prayed over this book, and I have faith that it will change your perspective and uplift you in those darkest moments.

In order for this book to help you, you must read *one* page per day.

Thank you for trusting me, and I hope you tune in for the books to come! I also have given others the chance to share their stories to give you encouragement.

Instagram platform: touchyournose_

To contact my father for words of encouragement, do the following:

1. Download JPay.
2. Find the inmate.
3. Florida Prison System.
4. DC# Y16046.
5. Ricardo Concepcion-Padilla.

INTRODUCTION

This book is a devotional-style book.

Pray the prayer I prayed in the beginning or a prayer of your own before reading this book *daily,* and have faith that God is doing something in your life.

Each piece of advice is a lesson I have learned from my father, who has been in prison for nineteen years of my life!

Each lesson was taken out of letters from my father over the years.

PRAY BEFORE YOU DIVE IN!

Heavenly Father, I come before you to thank you for this day that you have given me. Thank you for all the pain and struggle that are used to build my character. I ask you to open my mind, heart, ears, and soul to every single message in this book. I ask that you reveal the things that I need to work on and help me find my purpose if I haven't figured it out already. I ask you to soften my heart and keep me open to learning what you would like to teach me. Please protect my family, and help us all break these generational curses—together or separated. Thank you for bringing this book, *Humble Pain,* into my life. Nothing in life is a coincidence, and I believe this book is purposeful for me. Please forgive me for my sins, and open my eyes to what they are so that I don't repeat those sins.

In Jesus's name, I pray with love. Amen.

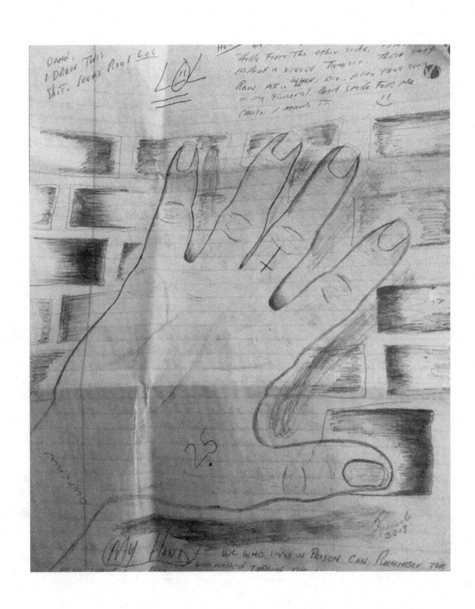

The happiness we receive from ourselves is greater
than what we obtain from our surroundings.
To be happy means to be self-sufficient.

What you put into your mind is what you will receive. It's an organism. Think positively, and think big. Don't harbor negative thoughts.

If they want to play the games with you, you'd better show 'em how it's done. You ain't nobody's fool.

The less you sleep, the more you accomplish.

Think, think, and think. Stop letting negativity throw
you off your game. I know it's hard, but you have one
thing that not many people have: freedom. Take advantage
of every good and bad situation. Learn, baby, learn.

Don't lose faith, and never let the vision of the prize leave your sight. Ever. When things in life don't go as planned and you're left dealing with life alone, take advantage and stay out of the mix.

When there is no loyalty, there is no foundation.

Get your plans ahead of you because you have a lot of dreams to accomplish, not for anybody but yourself.

Be consistent in life, and you'll prevail like the waves.

Goal equals locking yourself into a gigantic task that you nevertheless are able to master. In it, you could prove to yourself that you have grown in stature and become what you have long intended to be.

Don't allow negative energy to steal your joy, and
don't let the past bring down your spirit. If something
gets in your way, pray and have faith. Stay calm.

Love is a losing game. When your love is contrary
to one, believe the signs. If you don't, the tide will
always throw you back. Let it go, and let God.

Life is based on the type of person you are and how you overcome the challenges you're facing. Keep in mind self-care should always be number one. You have to take care of yourself first, by all means.

Seek the light, so the darkness can't bring you down.

Sex without marriage is not love. Instead,
it is the divorce from love.

You must be able to adapt to all of the situations life throws at you. You can't let hardships lead you to despair. You must continue and not abandon your mission.

Like Rick Ross says, "Cry only when babies die."

Mental health is an ongoing issue in our nation. Love can affect your daily life, physically and mentally. In that case, you have no room for toxic people. Being able to free yourself from those types of people is growth.

I have to stop! Pen, stop! Blame my hand, for it will eat a
pen in a day with its scribe. That's what happens when you're
locked in a cell for 365 days a year for life. The government
may think it may destroy me by keeping me segregated,
but one thing is for sure: my strength is in my seeds.
The same will go for you, regardless of where you are.

I have learned that going against the tide doesn't ever work.
Everything will eventually fall into place. Trust that there will
be ups and downs, as long as there are more ups than downs.

Love comes from the heart. It's natural, and it never lies.
Love's actions will always be stronger than words.

Learn to create art out of nothing.

Everybody has issues. Nobody is perfect. But
know that we can make a difference each and
every day, if we try. Take it day by day.

Faith is knowledge within the heart, beyond the reach of proof.

When somebody cares about you, he or she will get at you like a gnat. But be aware, and no matter what, you need to be the leader in the situation. You are not a remote control. You push your own buttons, making the best plays always.

Being kindhearted doesn't always get appreciated like you want it to. People tend to confuse that with weakness, but you have to be tough at all times. God knows our hearts and knows where we stand. People will respect you more when you're tough because they don't know what's going on inside you. Being in this cell, I'm surrounded by thousands of personalities daily, and I see how the strong prey off the weak. It's life. Show any kind of weakness, and the wolves will come and snatch it.

May you win the battle when it comes to your test of faith. You're always one decision away from making the man up above happy with you.

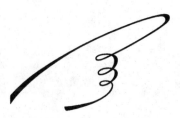

Do you plan out everything precisely? I believe it's important because if not, you'll let chance win. Remember that element of surprise is real. So be ready: guard always up and *never* down!

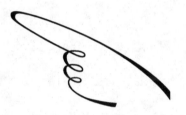

I believe in self-awareness; if you listen to that little voice in your head, you'll go far in life. Follow your intuition.

Bad things aren't happening to you;
great lessons are being learned.

If you don't believe in yourself, who will?

How they treat you is how they feel about you. Simple.

Put your faith in man, and he will fail you each and every time.

Some days, it's just better to handle things on your own.

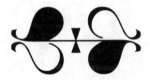

You are who you hang around, so surround yourself with bosses who accomplish things in life. Stay away from the ones who are just floating their lives away.

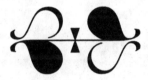

I don't care how much you love them. You need to love yourself
the most. You're the only one who's going to take care of you.

If you want to swim with piranhas, you're going
to get torn up. Protect your energy.

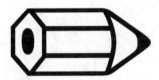

The type of parent you have really shapes the type of person you are. Misguidance, abuse, or full support can really affect a person. Be better than the ones who raised you—some way, somehow. You know what's right. Follow your spirit.

Love hurts. Love can cost your life. Stay away from it until you are at your fullest potential. There's a lot to learn.

Cherish your elders. They aren't here forever. They are disappearing faster than ever, taking your energy along with them. I don't think it ever gets easier.

Be a humble and innocent person. God is watching you
at all times, and you will have to face him in the end.

Spend more time with children because they are the future.

If they don't care about their own existence,
they won't care about you.

A peaceful work environment is rare,
so if you have it, appreciate it.

Smile times one hundred. Because you can.

When situations get hard, know that you
are breaking generational curses. Don't take
the easy route, but *face* it head-on.

No matter what, tell people how you're feeling. Speak, because the more you carry on the inside, the tougher the wall gets! Showing your emotions doesn't mean that you're a coward. No, it means that you understand yourself and you're letting the words out so that they can move mountains for you. No matter what the situation, speak up!

I hope you're having an amazing day, and if
you aren't, you'd better find a way.

Save your money. Bank it until you need it. Don't get too excited, because when you do, everything falls apart. That goes for everything. Never let your guard down. The day you do is the day you pay.

Always know that God has a plan. Keep your
faith, and keep working toward discovering your
purpose. We were all put here for a reason.

You keep doing your thing, and stay away from low-life people.
Know your ground, and stand for what you believe in.

Your past shouldn't worry you. Your future should.

Live your life, and stop worrying about the people who left you. They don't worry about you, so let it go. Do you.

Friends turn into foes in a heartbeat.

Be 360 degrees well-founded, and your
accomplishments will be amazing.

There's nothing wrong with helping people out.
Just make sure you're helping yourself out first
and that it doesn't drain all of your energy.

Life can treat us badly while growing up. But it's up to us to be the change in the generations to come. You must be the change.

Some people commit incestuous acts because they're not stable; they are led in the wrong paths. They possibly have seen too many sex movies as children and this sticks in their heads. Now they want to do the same to others. But because they're so young, they don't have anyone but their own family members around. So they conduct these acts on them. It's a tough thing to battle, but recognize it for what it is.

Family is more necessary to the happy than to the unhappy, for happiness is multiplied by being shared. It is more important than justice. For when you really find a friend in a family member, justice is unnecessary. A friend is one soul in two bodies.

You are an amazing person. When you say, "Jump,"
they're supposed to ask you, "How high?"

Your loyalty for one might not be the same for all.
And all might not be as loyal to you as for one.

Great minds are hard to kill.

Ask, and you will receive. Knock, and those doors will open.

You must be able to adapt to all the situations life throws at you. You can't let hardships lead you to despair. You must continue and not abandon your mission.

Look into the mirror, and remember who's the boss.

Never let someone think you need them. Stay bold.

Paint a picture with your words. They need *you*.

If people feed you rocks, feed them boulders.
If they feed you lamb, feed them steak.

Life laughs at suicide while it smiles at death. Why?
The smile knows you messed up, and it's going to bring
you back here in a position seven times worse.

Never put your mind so far out that you're thinking about getting rich but don't know how or what you're going to do to get there. Remember the money is always there. It's the works you have to worry about.

If you stay busy, you have no time to be depressed.

A weapon doesn't know feelings. Your words
are the most powerful weapons.

Just because you're going through a hard time
doesn't mean you are the only one. Take a look
at the bigger picture, and trust the process.

I know you're working on your future right now, and that's the main reason it's hard to put a smile on your face. I know it gets stressful, but relax and know that God has control of it all.

Appreciate all the things around you, and show your appreciation. You never know when the last time could be. I'm not saying you should think of that often. I think we should just live every day like it's our last.

Never stop appreciating those who brought
you in and treated you like family.

Years pass like waves in the ocean, so you'd
better enjoy them while you're young.

If they aren't here now, they never were.

Be the boss at everything you do, and keep your emotions out of it. We can't deal in emotion because dealing in emotions gets us in trouble. *One* thought may lead to destruction.

Leave negativity behind. I don't care how much money is involved. Money doesn't buy happiness. Instead, it may lead you in the wrong direction. Even billionaires aren't happy. Most people who commit suicide are billionaires. They're lonely, and money can't buy love or happiness.

Stop using your free time trying to prove your point to anyone. You don't owe anything to anyone but yourself.

Take care of yourself in all aspects of your life, so you don't put up with anyone who treats you otherwise.

Appreciate *everything*. Please. Be thankful you have a home to live in, food on the table, and family around you.

Life's ups and downs come and go. You must stay faithful
to the man up above, regardless of what happens.

If you're broke but you love your neighbor as you love yourself,
then you'll find a way. It doesn't matter the feedback. Don't
ever worry or focus on the feedback; just remain positive. Treat
people like you treat a child: with love, smiles, and laughter.

Invest in those who invest in you.

When things don't work out for you, it 100 percent was not supposed to work out. Always look at the bigger picture, and you will find the reason. Always remember that life is not understood forward but backward.

Time well spent is purposeful instead of reminiscing
about the people or things that are gone.

State your claim in a fashionable way.

Learn how to take control of every bad situation. You need to learn how to control those rainy days.

Watch your mouth. Your tongue is so small but so dangerous. It could put you in some messed-up situations. That doesn't mean for you to be scared to express how you feel. Focus on how you say it. You speak life or death.

Don't get involved in negativity. Always surround
yourself with positive people, places, and things.

Circumstances may be depressing, but you have to pull through because life goes on. Change your perspective so that your perspective doesn't change you.

Are you motivated? Are you moving your feet to
get the foundation started? Think about it.

Learn new ways, and create new magic in life.
You have the chance to prove to the world it's
yours! Tame it, or let it roar like a lion.

Want the best for yourself, and really seek
what God wants for your life.

Every bird must find a place to land.

If you continue to try pleasing the world, you will find yourself in a depression forever. Love yourself, and stop worrying about everyone else.

I consider a friend someone who is willing to listen to my awful words and move on them, for the better and not for the worse. If I'm helping them, let it be. Their smiles will show.

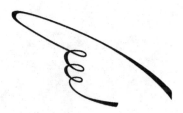

Just know my words have broken "happy homes," awful homes, and shady homes. I think it's my gift from God, but only time will tell. They say words move mountains.

I'm proud of you for being so tough that you don't break.
That's how you need to be toward any inconveniences in life.

Be loyal to who you are. You are who you are. God made you exactly how he wanted to. Don't change for anyone.

One of the most essential elements in winning any battle is through communication. That's the way any war is won.

Raise yourself up right, and strengthen your mind.

Tranquilita y dale gracias a la vida. Translation:
Calm down and be thankful for your life.

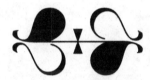

Loose lips sink ships. That's why you must mind
your own—unless someone's messing with you;
then by all means, it becomes your business.

Sometimes people don't deserve your pure heart. God will always be there to protect it *if* you let him. Pray about it.

Remind your parents and guardians how much you
love and appreciate them daily. They are facing their
own battles and countlessly blame themselves for life
lessons you may have faced. Remind them you wouldn't
be you without them, and give them a hug.

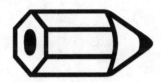

Love is stronger than blood.

Sometimes people just talk to talk. They have nothing better to do other than gossip about other people's lives. When they do that, leave their presence. They are no good for your health.

Reach for your dreams the same way you
reach for your phone in the morning.

Always have patience in life. Things will come to you like
a bee. It'll sting you at the right time. Be prepared for it.

Learn as much as you can from a person before you decide to give them some love. Learn how they treat their occupation, their people, their goals, etc. Their friendship will be more valuable in the end.

Love will bring you down; your vision will raise
you up. Love your vision, shower with your vision,
undress, and redress with it. You'll see how far you'll
go. Your vision won't die unless you divorce it.

Make no time for depression. Beat depression
with resistance. I don't care how much life beats
you. Be prepared for the toughest match.

Be as a baby and observe so that you can reconstruct
for a brighter way in this darkness.

Never be ashamed of the way you put food on your table.

You can't expect change if you don't move your feet. Get on it.

So what? Your mother wasn't a mom. So what? Your father wasn't in your life? Don't let these demons keep nagging at you. Confront them. *Let them go.*

If they don't appreciate you the first time around, stop telling yourself that they will the second time around.

There is no love in this world, baby. It's really hard
to find loyalty. It doesn't come around very often.
Don't trust so easily, and never leave your heart
in the air. Keep it tucked and out of sight.

Don't settle today. Strive for the best always. Every single day.

Words can build cities, and words can destroy them. Have faith when you speak your words. Speak *life*, not *death*.

Don't let the mistakes of others do you harm. Move forward.

Anxiety is your signal to pray.

Smile, and let the seasons come. I don't know if what I'm saying is reaching you. I just hope you know that life isn't pretty. Only the strong survive. Give yourself a hug, and smile.

Set boundaries, and let nobody come between those.

Nothing gets accomplished when you're
asleep. Physically or spiritually.

Never bring a child into this world without
building a foundation first.

Love yourself so when love comes, it isn't a stranger.

United we stand, and divided we fall.

When we stop blaming others for our
lifestyles, we move forward.

When you plan, you achieve.

The pain and suffering are going to keep you strong in life. You have to make it through the worst just to get to heaven. When the Bible talks about Jesus, and when Jesus was hung on the cross, the pain and suffering he went through were inhumane. He even asked His Father, "Why have you forsaken me?" (Matthew 27:46 NIV; Mark 15:34 NIV). The pain was great, but according to the Bible, he made it and rose again. Now millions of people call upon his name for mercy and forgiveness in life. There're always going to be stumbling blocks/headaches/heartaches in anything you do, but those tornadoes and storms are what built you.

Get a schedule going, and never deviate from it! The moment you deviate from that schedule is the moment you have to open your third eye so that you can see destruction coming. Try it out. See how making a schedule in your life will meet ends always.

Remember your mistakes, and value your ways.

Be smart, be patient, and have good company.
When I say "company," I mean God and those he
has put into your life for good and not evil.

Learn how to avoid adapting to ways that put you in unhealthy situations. That way, you can advance in life as you go.

A man built of wisdom is more powerful
than a man built from money.

Be excellent in knowledge and wisdom because those
are the things that give life to those who have them.
So keep them close, and they will carry you far.

There's no better journey than the journey of purpose.

It's either "I love you" or "I hate you." There is no in-between. If I hate you, it's because you sparked that in me for whatever reason.

One mistake can destroy the lives of generations to come.

RICARDO'S FAVORITE SONGS

- "Hello" by Adele (funeral song)
- "Ferrari Rojo" by Bulova, Jaudy, and RC La Sensacion (birthday song)
- "Hope" by Ace Hood (dedicated to me)
- "Moment 4 Life" by Drake and Nicki Minaj
- "Cold Hearted II" by Meek Mill

Printed in the United States
By Bookmasters